Portsmouth

— A SHATTERED CITY —

Anthony Triggs

HALSGROVE

First published in Great Britain in 2003
Reprinted 2007
Copyright © 2003 Anthony Triggs

British Library Cataloguing-in-Publication Data
A CIP record for this title is available from the British Library

ISBN 978 1 84114 318 7

HALSGROVE
Halsgrove House
Ryelands Farm Industrial Estate
Bagley Green, Wellington
Somerset TA21 9PZ
Tel: 01823 653777
Fax: 01823 216796
email: sales@halsgrove.com
website: www.halsgrove.com

Printed and bound in Great Britain
by The Cromwell Press, Trowbridge

Acknowledgements

As always I would like to thank my publisher, Steven Pugsley, and all the staff at Halsgrove for their help. I must also say thank you to Keely Storey, Alf Harris, and my wife Sue who always gives her unfailing support; and finally the unknown photographers from the 1940s who made this collection possible.

The Author

Anthony Triggs is the author of twelve previous books about the history of the Portsmouth area. He is a retired *News* journalist and lives at Portchester with his wife Sue.

Introduction

he old city of Portsmouth took a battering during the Second World War. The proximity of Spithead and the Solent made it a sure target, but the dockyard and numerous industrial premises added to the fears of residents when war was declared in September 1939 that the city would not escape the Luftwaffe's attentions.

The city fathers prepared for the worst and the Portsmouth War Emergency Committee was set up, and civic workers were moved from the Guildhall to other areas as a precaution.

However, it was not until 11 July 1940 that the first German bombs hit the city. Heinkel pilots overshot their target of the dockyard and their bombs landed devastatingly in the area of Kingston. The first bomb fell near the Blue Anchor public house and others damaged a city landmark, the Rudmore gasholder. Altogether 20 bombs hit the city and dozens of buildings were destroyed. In August a daylight raid ended with the destruction of Portsmouth Harbour railway station and the church of St John in Prince George Street. Later in the month Southsea became the target and much of the Kings Road shopping area was damaged, but far worse was to come. On the dreadful night of Friday 10 January 1941, one of the greatest attacks left much of the old city in ruins. Three hundred raiders dropped 25,000 incendiaries and numerous high-explosive bombs, and at one time 28 major fires were burning, with no effective water supply to tackle them. The magnificent Guildhall was destroyed, as was Clarence Pier, the Eye and Ear Hospital, the Hippodrome Theatre, the Connaught Drill Hall in Stanhope Road, the Central Hotel, and part of the Royal Hospital. The attack left 3000 people homeless, 430 were injured and more than 170 lost their lives.

After the war ended Portsmouth was faced with the enormous problem of recovery from the ravages of the blitz, and to help the effort the *Evening News* produced an evocative reminder of the terrible times the city had endured. It was called *Smitten City*, and its stark red and black cover made sure the book became a best seller, bringing in much-needed funds to the city. As the years went by the book became a collectors' item and eventually *The News*, as the *Evening News* was then called, published a reprint in 1981.

Although the pictures contained in *Smitten City* show the terrible devastation visited upon Portsmouth, it was published before the big clean-up began: before the derelict houses were removed, before dangerous walls were destroyed, and before the bomb-sites were cleared of unsightly rubble.

This new collection of rare images aims to redress the situation by bringing to readers a unique pictorial record of the streets and roads of a shattered city after the bulldozers and trucks had done their work. It shows the familiar streets with the giant gaps where once stood homes, shops, churches, schools and theatres, all awaiting the coming of the builders, all awaiting the arrival of the new peacetime Portsmouth.

Anthony Triggs,
Portchester, 2003

The Blue Anchor at Kingston Cross was the first casualty of the war when the bombs hit a surprised city on 11 July, 1940.

The Keppel's Head Hotel, named after Admiral Augustus Keppel, is on the right of this postcard view of The Hard. Because of its proximity to the dockyard much of this area took a beating during the blitz.

This view is taken from almost the same position as that adopted by the unknown camera-man who secured the earlier picture. Now this desolate view shows the line of old buildings boarded and propped up.

The view today shows how modern development has changed the area with The Hard Interchange and the tourist activity of the visitors to *Victory, Warrior* and *Mary Rose.*

The Keppel's Head takes centre stage again flanked by the ruins of the Row Barge public house, which stood on the corner of College Street.

The Hard is pictured here in those balmy peacetime days before the two terrible wars were to change countless lives.

Gentlemen's outfitters Moss Bros display their elegant wares in the company's newly-built brick building at The Hard, which replaced its earlier temporary home in a wooden hut. The café next door is utilising a Nissen hut. This ubiquitous form of building was invented by British army officer and mining engineer, Peter Norman Nissen.

The dockyard main gate is pictured in those quieter Victorian times when everyone wore a hat and most ladies carried a parasol, although the brave young thing on the left of the picture is obviously expecting fine weather as she has hers in the rolled-up position.

The German bombs made sure that Totterdell's Family Hotel closed for business on a permanent basis. The hotel stood in St George's Square and boasted – if the sign is any indication – that it had been established in the mid 1800s. Behind the hotel can be seen the ruins of the Eagle Tavern.

Two boarded-up public houses – the Duke of Edinburgh and The Keys – are pictured here in Lennox Row, which ran into Flathouse Road, Portsea.

Brewing has always been an important industry in Portsmouth and a great loss was the St George Brewhouse, seen here looking skeletal and derelict.

Demolition crews make safe the bombed area of St George's Square. To the left of the picture is the well-known St George's Hotel, which was one of a great number of places in the square where liquid refreshment could be obtained in pre-war times. The famous novelist Sir Walter Besant was born in St George's Square.

This moody view from the main gate of the dockyard looking up Queen Street is strangely reminiscent of a picture from a northern industrial town.

Before the war Queen Street – named after Queen Anne – was a bustling thoroughfare linking the dockyard and naval base with the town.

Timothy White's store is seen on the corner of Cross Street to the extreme right of this picture of Queen Street. The chemists and hardware chain was founded in Portsmouth in 1848 and by the 1920s had spread its branches over much of southern England. It was eventually taken over by Boots in 1968 in a deal worth £35m.

Another street corner in Queen Street presents a bleak look. Shops are boarded up with gaps where dangerous brickwork has already been removed. The poster on the wall is exhorting people to buy war bonds.

This picture, taken shortly after the previous one, shows the same corner after the clearance teams had done their work. The site has been cleared, and with temporary fencing installed, it looks quite tidy.

The flats in St Nicholas Street provided a wonderful viewpoint for a photographer who wanted a slightly different look at this part of Portsea. The dockyard is in the background. In the distance is the distinctive cupola of the Old Naval Academy. The Academy was built in 1733 and was the first naval training shore establishment in the country. On the extreme right of the picture can be seen the huge buildings of the Brickwoods Brewery.

Clarence Street ran off Queen Street and contained many early Georgian-style properties, as can be seen by the one left standing at the extreme left of the picture.

Clarence Street takes a photo-call again while demolition is under way, removing the remains of the last of the street's historic houses.

The Edinburgh Road store of naval and military publishers Gale and Polden is boarded up on the corner of Stanhope Road in this view down towards Commercial Road taken in 1946.

The white-painted trees near the Roman Catholic Cathedral in Edinburgh Road bear witness to the blackout regulations that were in force during the war years.

The rubble is being cleared from Fountain Street, which was named after the old Fountain Well that once stood on the site. The Shipwright's Arms, on the corner of Fountain Street and Edinburgh Road, was a popular watering hole for the crowds leaving the Empire Palace Theatre, which was situated right opposite.

The cast takes a photo-call outside the ornate frontage of the Empire Palace Theatre in the days before the war.

After the Guildhall was gutted in the blitz the area around the huge building was fenced off as a safety precaution. Life had to continue and people are pictured here waiting for buses and going about their normal business. Across the square the Sussex Hotel stands on the corner of Greetham Street, all of which is now covered by the Civic Office complex.

The site of the old Hippodrome Theatre is an empty space on the right of the picture in this evocative view from the steps of the Guildhall. This was the last of the bomb-sites to be redeveloped, and the old 'Hipp' is now remembered by an office block called Hippodrome House. The site did not give up its secrets easily. On 12 October 1984 workmen on the site uncovered a 500lb unexploded bomb and the city centre was evacuated. American entertainer Bob Hope was due to appear at the Guildhall but the show had to be cancelled. From that time the incident has always been known as the 'Bob Hope bomb.'

Teams of servicemen were pulled in for duty clearing the rubble from the gutted Guildhall, doing most of the work with hand tools and wooden wheelbarrows.

After the bombing it was many weeks before the shell of the Guildhall was cool enough to be entered, when it was discovered that the muniment rooms, containing the city plate and lord mayor's regalia, had survived the blaze. The building, which was opened in 1890, was rebuilt after the war, and here scaffolding surrounds one of the minaret towers while the work is undertaken.

In June 1953 the Guildhall was given a new look – albeit temporary – when the city celebrated the coronation of the Queen. It was to be another six years before the sovereign came to Portsmouth to perform the opening ceremony on 8 June, 1959.

The Connaught Drill Hall in Stanhope Road became a casualty of war on the night of 10 January, 1941, although the offices of the *Evening News*, in the background, escaped relatively unscathed. The hall was opened on 9 March, 1901. The Zurich Insurance building now stands on the *Evening News* site.

The rebuilt Connaught Drill Hall looks smart and new as it awaits its official reopening. In the background to the right of this picture can be seen the top of the Empire Palace Theatre in Edinburgh Road.

On 20 July, 1951, crowds gathered in the city to welcome Princess Elizabeth. She was visiting Portsmouth to open the new United Services Officers' Club and the rebuilt Connaught Drill Hall in Stanhope Road, where crowds are pictured awaiting the royal visitor. The princess took a 7-mile tour of the city and at some places the crowds were so great that eventually the royal procession was ten minutes late.

The *Evening News* HQ in Stanhope Road continued to operate until 1969 when the newspaper moved to its new purpose-built premises at Hilsea, where it utilised leading-edge computer technology to produce the paper, which was then renamed *The News*.

The imposing Central Hotel stood on the corner of Commercial Road and Edinburgh Road, and because of its situation became a popular venue for visitors who had come to the city by train.

A police officer stands on point duty outside the ruins of the Central Hotel. By this time the important city centre site was up for auction for redevelopment.

The Central Hotel can be seen in the distance on the corner of Edinburgh Road in this view across the area that once housed Commercial Road shops.

Work starts on the reconstruction of the Landport Drapery Bazaar store site in Commercial Road. The store was rebuilt and reopened in 1954, and in 1965 was bought by the United Drapery Group, changing its name to Allders in 1982. The Empire Theatre can be seen in Edinburgh Road along with the Barclays Bank building on the corner.

After the war the Landport Drapery Bazaar took its organisation to many smaller temporary premises scattered around the city, such as this one in Kingston Road.

Even with no real central premises the Landport Drapery Bazaar managed to celebrate its eightieth birthday with a fashion show at the Savoy ballrooms at South Parade.

This part of the city was a thriving shopping and banking area before the war. In this scene Edinburgh Road is running out towards the left of the picture, while Commercial Road – now a pedestrian precinct – runs out to the right.

Life goes on as normal on the junction of Commercial Road and Edinburgh Road. In the middle can be seen H. Samuel's and the Classic Cinema.

The clear site in the centre of the picture is home to a notice proclaiming the area to be the new Woolworth's store. In the background to the right of the picture is St Agatha's Church, which still stands in the city today.

This view northwards along Commercial Road shows the damage wrought by the blitz. The cameraman is standing in Chandos Street and the road leading out to the right of the picture is Buckingham Street.

The enterprising cameraman has adopted a higher viewpoint, aiming his lens on Commercial Road from an upper window of H. Samuel's jewellery store. Scaffolding is already in place as rebuilding commences. Opposite Arundel Street is the ornate frontage of Lloyds Bank.

The C&A store in Commercial Road reopened in 1950. The banner on the storefront is advertising the event. The store became a large employer in the city with its factory at Paulsgrove.

By 1953 the store was gaily decorated for the coronation, an event that gave a colourful boost to a country that was still reeling after wartime austerity.

The awning of the Classic Cinema, opened in September 1936 originally as Cinenews, is to the extreme left of this post-war view of Commercial Road. The corner of Meadow Street can just be seen near the parked van. The shops on the right of the picture were re-developed after the war, and today the area on the left is part of the Cascades Centre.

Charlotte Street was a bustling and busy market for many years, but was much damaged during the war. However, the patriotic spirit is still apparent as shown by the Union Flag draped over the barrier.

The camera has now moved to the other end of Charlotte Street at its junction with Commercial Road. An interested pass-er-by stops to look at the piles of rubble and timber on an area which was once a busy store. The public house on the corner is the Monarch.

The intrepid photographer has returned to the same place in Charlotte Street to record the scene a short while later. The area has been cleared and looks quite tidy, so much in fact that a motorist has already decided to use the space as a car park. Lake Road, with the unusual-shaped roof of the Employment Exchange, can be seen in the distance.

Charlotte Street in the '70s still retained its busy atmosphere but with nothing like the character of its pre-war days.

This view from upon high across Charlotte Street shows two of the most frequented places in past times almost sandwiched together: the church and the pub. In the background is the beautiful church of St Agatha with the Golden Bell in seemingly close proximity

Pedestrians and cyclists pass the ornate frontage of the City Buildings on the corner of Commercial Road and Lake Road, once home to a number of shops and offices.

The cameraman takes a longer shot a few weeks later and records the open space where the City Buildings used to stand. To the right is the Emperor of India public house that reopened after the war but was eventually demolished in the '60s.

Lake Road, formerly Lake Lane, was once a busy street of tiny shops selling a huge variety of goods: in the aftermath of the bombing it looks a poor reflection of its former hustle and bustle.

The sad remains of the Sultan public house stand on the corner of Alexandra Street and Lake Road. Just past the public house can be seen the ornate frontage of the Princes Theatre. The Princes was originally a theatre but became a cinema in 1924; it became a victim of the blitz in January 1941 when it was hit during a children's Saturday afternoon matinee.

Lake Road was realigned with the regeneration of the city after the war. Although the then recently rebuilt Tramway Arms public house still stands, Lake Road's junction with Kingston Road is now further to the south.

The Tramway Arms today provides a strange impression with the blank rear wall where once stood the tiny shops of Lake Road.

The Black Dog public house is on the left of this picture of Arundel Street at the Fratton Road end. To the right is Besant Road, and to the left is St John's Road. On the opposite corner stand the sad remains of the Fratton Street School.

The school is pictured here at its junction with Spencer Road (now Murfield Road) and Arundel Street. It is interesting to wonder whether the children in the picture were former pupils.

Atterbury's chemists shop once provided a service to the community from its popular position on the corner of Somers Road and Bradford Road. Now it is just one part of another shopping area lost to the city.

The cranes are at work in Raglan Street. To the right a Brickwoods Sunshine Ales sign indicates the position of the street's only pub, the Raglan.

The gutted ruin of the once-beautiful St Paul's Church shows up on the horizon to the left of this unusual panorama from Southsea Terrace.

The tower of the gutted Guildhall and that of the Technical College behind it dominate this view across Hyde Park Road as the demolition crews fill the huge crane buckets with rubble.

The cameraman adopts the same viewpoint a few weeks later and records the site looking tidy and safe.

The Guildhall stands in the distance overlooking the desolation of Middle Street, which ran from Sackville Street to Hyde Park Road.

The Hyde Park Road area became popular in the '50s and '60s when it was the location of the bus and coach terminus, as this picture shows. In the '70s, with the complete redevelopment of the Guildhall area its character disappeared and another part of the city's past was lost.

The cars standing in the parking area near Liningtons car sales premises look strangely out of place in the almost moon-like landscape of the Russell Street area. In the background at the centre of the picture is the Wellington Hall where hundreds of Portsmouth people, including the author, learned the rudiments of ballroom dancing.

Regulars at the Three Stags in Russell Street would have been forced to find another place to drink after their local – seen on the left of the picture – was destroyed. The street running out to the right of the picture is Salem Street, which today is Dorothy Dymond Street, just a short cul-de-sac behind Hippodrome House.

The poor old Three Stags can be seen in the centre of this shot of Russell Street taken from the corner of Upper Swan Street. The Tudor look of the White Swan public house can just be seen in Commercial Road at the end of Swan Street. Swan Street has now been renamed Alec Rose Lane and that part of Commercial Road is now Guildhall Walk.

Pye Street ran off Charlotte Street, parallel with Commercial Road. It still exists today although in a rather truncated form near the Tricorn Centre, itself destined to become a thing of the past.

Pye Street today is just a shadow of its former self, just visible from Market Way.

These are the sad remains of the Southsea Brewery in Hambrook Street after the bombs had reduced it to rubble. Barrels and crates can be seen piled in the yard – what a blow to Portsmouth pubgoers!

Palmer's Brewery stood in King Street and produced beer for many of the small public houses and beer houses in Portsea.

Portsmouth, being a naval city, was home to a number of breweries. Brickwoods, Longs, and Pike Spicer were some of the more well-known names. Portsmouth and Brighton United Breweries ran the Crown Brewery in Clarendon Street, although the premises here are sadly up for sale.

The wide-open spaces of King Street show graphically how the war completely changed the face of Portsmouth.

The Avenue takes on a country air – to go with its pastoral name – with the fine trees and the four-wheeled cart loaded with unwanted timber.

North Street was one of the small thoroughfares of Portsea and ran between Queen Street and Lennox Row. Again the barriers have been erected as a safety precaution – not only to stop children injuring themselves, but possibly to stop the unwary pubgoers from falling in while on their way home on a Friday night.

Britain Street, the birthplace of Isambard Kingdom Brunel, has the wreckers in, removing the dangerous brickwork from a block of flats, once home to many Portsea inhabitants. Brunel's original home is sadly no more but his birthplace is now marked with a commemorative stone.

Prince George Street at Portsea, once home to many Portmuthians, takes on the look of the wide-open spaces in this evocative picture taken in the late 1940s.

This second view of Prince George Street showing the space in the foreground where once stood the church of St John the Evangelist. The church, which for many years was the home of the well-known fire-and-brimstone vicar the Rev. Henry Lindsay Young, was destroyed in that terrible series of raids in January 1941.

The church of St John dated from 1789 and was built mainly of timber. Once the flames took hold there was nothing to be done, the valiant efforts of the fire crews were in vain and another of Portsmouth's historic buildings was lost.

Blackfriars Road, originally called Canal View, looks sad with the ruins of shops and homes to the left of the picture. On the right is Alpha Street.

The Kent Street Chapel was another religious building that was destroyed in the war. The Gothic-style building was erected in 1847 and cost £4000 – a huge amount in those times. In 1891 the building was destroyed by fire and it was rebuilt to the same design, only to be lost again during the war.

Rebuilding starts on these homes in Olinda Street and the piles of bricks indicate the task ahead. The policeman on his bike takes a photo-call.

Kings Road was a favourite shopping centre before the war with many popular shops and department stores. This FGO Stuart postcard shows the area on what is obviously a hot day if the shop blinds are any indication.

This is Kings Road following the 1941 attack, showing the desolation and damage inflicted on the city. What was once a thriving shopping area is now a blackened ruin.

St James's Road, seen here at its junction with Brougham Road, was situated between two of the hardest-hit areas of the city – Kings Road and St Paul's.

York Street and Hyde Street were also in the firing line when the Kings Road shopping area was hit, bringing devastation and homelessness to many residents.

A market trader has set up his stall in Kent Road, Southsea, against the imposing background of Thomas Ellis Owen's St Jude's Church. Many traders used these sites to set up new businesses or to continue their pre-war occupation following the destruction of their homes and shops.

The Eye and Ear Hospital took a beating in January 1941. The photographer has recorded the desolate sight of what was left of an institution that existed only to care for people in need.

Palmerston Road assumes an unusual look after much of the remains of the bombed shops were removed. Marmion Road is to the left of the picture, while Kent Road runs out to the right.

In an attempt to make the larger bomb-sites less of an eyesore the city fathers had a number converted into temporary gardens. These gardens are on the site of the Handleys department store, which was destroyed during the 10 January, 1941 raids. Like the Landport Drapery Bazaar the store managed to trade from a number of temporary premises until the premises were rebuilt and reopened in 1955. The store is now part of the Debenhams empire.

Parents and children take a short cut through the temporary gardens, overlooked by the desolation wrought by the bombing.

The area around Alhambra Road at Southsea was hit badly with many homes lost. This picture shows some of the ruins before the big tidy-up.

How different is this second picture showing the same area after is was cleared of rubble and bombed buildings.

Collett and Collett's auction galleries in Castle Road would be holding no more sales following the January 1941 attacks.

Moving round the city to Old Portsmouth the desolation is evident behind this old gentleman as he takes a short cut near the Hot Walls.

The Cathedral of St Thomas was originally situated behind a line of buildings that were destroyed in the war, allowing for the Cathedral Green to be developed.

Portsmouth Cathedral stands proudly amid the rubble. Temporary barriers were erected at bomb-sites all around the city as a safety precaution.

The rear view of the City Museum, once the Old Town Hall, with its high portico, can be seen from Penny Street as the camera is trained across High Street to the Cathedral.

The Cathedral spire is dominant in this view of High Street with Pembroke Road running in at the bottom left of this high-level picture. The slopes of Portsdown Hill can be clearly seen in the distance.

A nice collection of early cars makes an interesting foreground to the ruined shops of High Street.

Today the Cathedral presents a pleasant outlook and is a popular attraction.

High Street, Old Portsmouth, taken from a high viewpoint clearly shows the vacant space on the right where once stood the old coaching inn, the George Hotel, famous for being the last place Nelson stayed before he left these shores for Trafalgar and immortality.

The George Hotel garage is recorded here before the war. The plaque on the wall tells of Nelson's final visit. The room in which he stayed was preserved until finally the German bombs removed another piece of Portsmouth's history.

Oyster Street is in the foreground of this view of the Hot Walls with Vospers yard in the centre of the picture. Fort Blockhouse can be seen across the harbour mouth at Gosport.

The overhead trolley bus lines make an interesting pattern at Cambridge Junction. High Street, with Portsmouth Grammar School, is on the extreme left of the picture, and White and Company's removals office is on the right, backed by the chimneys of the power station. The sailors take centre stage as they survey the damage.

The huge amounts of rubble from the bombed buildings were collected and stored in dumps around the city. There were three major sites: one at Baffins, one near the ruined St Paul's Church, and one at Conway Street where dozens of tiny homes were flattened in one air raid. This evocative picture shows the huge pile of bricks at the Conway Street dump.

Truck drivers await instructions for unloading their cargoes at the Baffins dump, watched with interest by a schoolboy.

A lorry tips its load of rubble on to the rapidly growing pile at the Baffins site.

A similar situation is under way as trucks disgorge their loads at the dump near St Paul's Church in Southsea.

One of the four huge pinnacles of St Paul's Church forms an interesting background to the more mundane work going on at the dump below. The beautiful church, which dated from 1820, was destroyed in the 10 January, 1941 attack when the entire interior – with the exception of the brass lectern – was lost.

Much of the hardcore was taken across the harbour to Gosport where it was used in the rebuilding of Portsmouth's sister town, which also suffered badly from the attentions of the German bombers. A number of lorries are seen here leaving Point on the floating bridge *Alexandra* for the short journey across the harbour.

Pictured from the Gosport side the loaded trucks are seen leaving the *Alexandra* on their way to the brick dumps in Gosport.

You could be forgiven for thinking that this final picture is from the 1940s or 1950s, but you would be wrong. The year is 1987 and much of the land around the western side of Commercial Road is being cleared for the eventual construction of the Cascades Shopping Centre, bringing another huge change to Portsmouth city centre.